A
BRAND-NEW
Butterfly

The monarch butterfly starts life as a tiny egg.

After about three days,
a tiny caterpillar hatches
out of the egg.

Slowly the caterpillar turns
yellow, black, and white.

The caterpillar eats all day long.
As it grows bigger, its skin
becomes tighter.

When the caterpillar's skin
gets too tight, it sheds it.
A new skin is underneath.

Soon the caterpillar can
grow no more.
It stops eating and hangs
upside down.

The caterpillar sheds its skin
for the very last time.
Underneath is a new skin.
This will become
the caterpillar's chrysalis.

The caterpillar will rest
inside the chrysalis.

Over the next twelve to fourteen days, it will slowly change into a monarch butterfly.

During its last week
in the chrysalis, you can see
the colors of the new butterfly.

Soon the chrysalis splits open.

Slowly and carefully
the monarch butterfly crawls out
of the chrysalis.

Its wings unfold as its body
pumps special fluid into them.

The monarch butterfly opens
its beautiful new wings.
It flaps them gently to dry them.
Soon it will be ready to fly.

A brand-new monarch butterfly has been formed.